SUPREME TEAMS

HOW TO MAKE TEAMS REALLY WORK

TEAM PROCESS AND DYNAMICS HANDBOOK
By Peter Capezio

National Press Publications endorses non-sexist language. In an effort to make this handbook clear, consistent and easy to read, we've used "he" throughout the odd-numbered chapters and "she" throughout the even-numbered chapters. The copy is not intended to be sexist.

Supreme Teams
Published by National Press Publications, Inc.
Copyright 1996 National Press Publications, Inc.
A Division of Rockhurst College Continuing Education Center, Inc.

Printed in the United States of America

1 2 3 4 5 6 7 8 9 10

ISBN 1-55852-171-2

SUPREME TEAMS
HOW TO MAKE TEAMS REALLY WORK

Introduction

Anyone two years old or older knows that people don't always act the way we think they should. People sometimes act in ways that contradict our expectations. When our different expectations aren't met, we can become confused, frustrated and even angry. Conflict often is the result when people have different expectations.

As a professional in the 90s, you must work closely with more people than ever. On the job, teams are a lot more common these days; getting results working with others is a challenge, especially when the team is diverse and varied. As a team member, you're charged with satisfying your customers and ensuring that all deadlines are met and results meet standards.

One powerful way to avoid confusion, frustration and conflict when working with others is to agree on what is mutually important to you and on how you want to work together. Discussing motives, why people do what they do and what each team member expects of the others helps create positive relationships. Team members can then focus their attention on optimal performance: getting work done faster, with better quality and for less cost.

The most successful teams achieve their best results by using optimal contributions of all the individual team members. When the team becomes stronger than the sum of the individual members, it achieves what is called "synergy." This may be the single most important key to building winning teams.

So how do you achieve synergy on your team? How can you establish positive relationships with your co-workers? What are the real paybacks if you are successful? How does one begin?

The answers to these questions may mean survival for many companies and their employees. By finding the answers for yourself, you'll be better prepared to be successful in the changing workplace. So sit back and get ready for a practical education on working successfully with others. You'll be glad you did. So will your co-workers.

1 WHY TEAMS?

During the 1980s, many changes occurred across American industry. These changes involved massive restructuring, which led to downsizing and layoffs. The survivors have found themselves in a new working environment — one that has fewer resources available (both people and financial) and less hierarchy in terms of jobs. The term "flatten" often has been used to describe the removal of layers of management now considered unnecessary to get the job done.

Other terms, such as "getting close to the customer," "empowering people," "speed to market" and "teams — all kinds of teams" are the new buzzwords in the language of business.

The teams you are most likely to be a part of have a variety of names. These are the most common types of teams:

- Cross-functional teams

- Corrective action teams

- Customer satisfaction teams

- Supplier relations teams

- Self-directed teams

- Continuous improvement teams

- and more!

Types of Teams

Teams have many names, but in general they fit into four major types:

- **Natural work teams** are made up of individuals who are based in the same work unit or share a function. They must rely on working together to produce the results expected for their department. The purchasing department is a good example of this type of team.

- **Cross-functional teams** are made up of individuals who represent several different departments or functions. They often work on projects that combine job functions. They need to plan, communicate and implement together to ensure that work is completed. In this type of team, you must watch the "hand-offs" or the exchanges between departments or functions. This is where many cross-functional teams fail because they don't have shared goals or don't consider the needs of the other department or function.

- **Corrective action teams (CATs)** are made up of individuals who come together for a given time to solve specific organizational problems. They may reside in a single work unit or be comprised of individuals from multiple departments. They usually have a formal beginning and disband after they present recommendations to a problem. Some CATs may then go on to become involved in corrective implementation.

- **Hybrid teams** are made up of individuals who may volunteer or form independently to work on a specific process improvement, which may lead to improved quality and productivity. These ad hoc teams fill in the gaps that other teams may not be assigned to cover.

One discovery from all of these organizational changes has been that employee teams can provide a competitive advantage. They create a horizontal network that crosses departmental lines and allows decisions to be made more quickly — by those closest to the work and the customer.

What is a team? To clearly understand how to make a team effective, it is important to start with a working definition of "team."

Team Definition: A group of individuals working together for a common purpose, who must rely on each other to achieve mutually defined results.

In reviewing the definition, think about a team you recently worked on. What was most difficult: defining the purpose and task or developing the working relationships in order to facilitate teamwork?

The most frequent response to this question is that effective relationships are most difficult to develop. Because we tend to function more easily as individuals, building relationships takes extra effort.

Increased Use of Employee Involvement and Teams

One major discovery has been the realization that employees can actually solve problems on the job! No longer are workers expected to check their "thinking caps" at the door on their way into work. As a result, there has been a dramatic increase in the use of employees — their ideas and suggestions — during the past century. Understanding the impact of employee involvement on productivity came through the work of Elton Mayo, Douglas McGregor and G. Edwards Deming, among many others. As employees become more involved on teams, new trends and implications are emerging in the workplace.

Increasing Employee Involvement and Teams

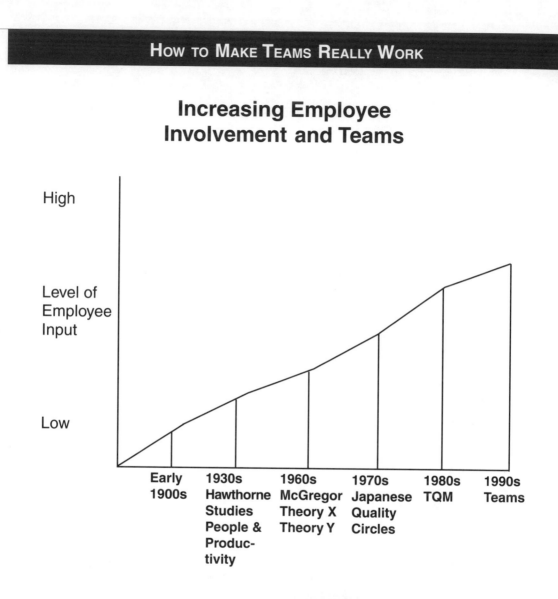

Trends and implications

- The company of the future will have fewer levels of authority and fewer resources available. This will result in fewer opportunities for advancement into management or supervisory positions. But it will also result in greater opportunities to make decisions and manage your own work environment.

4

- Enormous competitive demands on companies will result in extraordinary pressure to obtain maximum productivity from every employee. Employees will have an increasing opportunity to contribute to their company's success.

- New technology changes will put more information in more people's hands faster. As distribution of information increases, more people will be expected to join in decision-making and creating options, and they will assume greater responsibilities. Employees will then become more positive and productive.

- Employees will not be assigned specific jobs, but increasingly they will become members of teams with specific results. The types and numbers of teams used in companies will increase dramatically over time.

The implications of these trends have great potential for you. As a key individual in your company, consider the opportunities for advancement that will come in the form of increased accountability in your current job, increased project responsibilities and a rise in individual empowerment. The challenge for you will be to build your skills in the areas of communications, problem-solving and decision-making. Most importantly, you'll need to learn to be a team player, one who is able to work effectively in teams with mutually accountable goals.

The employees who are most successful in this new environment will have opportunities to participate in many efforts. This participation will increase in scope and responsibility. Opportunities to lead team efforts will be plentiful, and effective team leaders will be critical to the success of most organizations.

As an individual developing in the team-based environment, you will be expected to become part of your organization's "family." You will be expected to "buy in" and support the company's values and goals. Performance expectations will increase, and feedback from customers will help determine your performance effectiveness. Average performers will be expected to "step up" their level of productivity. Poor performers may not have enough ability or motivation to keep up with the basic requirements of their jobs.

Rethinking Values

As a result of the changing workplace, you will be required to rethink your work values. Review the shift in work values and plan to revise your role in your organization. This will be an important step in adjusting to the new performance expectations.

Old Ways	New Ideas
My boss pays my salary. I may talk about serving the customer, but the real objective is to keep the boss happy.	Customers pay our salaries. We must do whatever it takes and work with whomever we can to please the customer.
I'm just a cog in the wheel. My best strategy is to keep my head down and not make waves.	Every job is essential and important. We get paid for the value we create and the relationships we build.
If something goes wrong, I dump the problem onto someone else. Why be identified with troubles?	The buck stops here. I must accept ownership of the problem and get it solved, accessing any resources I can find.
The more direct reports I have, the more important I am. The one with the biggest empire wins.	I belong to a team: We fail or succeed together, and if we fail, nobody's empire is a winner.
Tomorrow will be just like today. It has always been, so the company's past tells me all I need to know.	Nobody knows what tomorrow holds. Constant learning is part of my job, customer service is my focus and cooperation a mandate.

Consider these action steps to help guide your behavior:

1. Find out why something is being done the way it is. Think about a way it can be done better, quicker or with less cost.

2. Be open minded. Don't make premature judgments.

3. Identify your main customers and suppliers. Learn their requirements and communicate your needs to them.

4. Be flexible. If one approach leads to a dead end, switch to another. Use as many perspectives as possible.

5. Be persistent. Take a shot at a problem each day. If you can't find a solution, forget the problem for a while, but return to it later.

6. Listen to your co-workers' problems about the details of their jobs. You may be able to provide an objective point of view because you're not directly involved.

7. Learn from the best. Someone else's idea may lead to one of your own.

For you to be successful, you will need to consider the types of teams in your organization and what your personal goals are for participating on them. To begin the process of identifying teams in your organization, it is important to understand the team expectations that exist. When you understand the types of teams operating around you, you'll be able to make a better judgment of how you can successfully participate.

Team Expectations

Quite often the expectations of teams are defined in terms of the results or outputs of their work. Some common measures include speed, cost and quality.

- *Speed:* The ability to deliver the product or service to the customer faster than the competition or respond to fixing a problem quickly

- *Quality:* The ability to meet or exceed the customer's expectations regarding the features and benefits of the product or service

- *Cost:* The ability to produce the product or service at a cost customers are willing to pay and which contributes to profitability

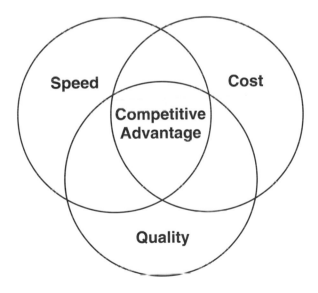

When speed, cost and quality are achieved together, they create a competitive advantage. This is a new way of thinking and breaks the old paradigm:

Speed, Cost, Quality — Pick Any Two

The old paradigm suggests that you can't have all three. For example:

"I can give you speed and build in

quality for a new product, but I can't

meet your cost requirements."

or

"I can give you speed and meet your cost

requirements, but I can't guarantee quality."

or

"I can meet your cost and quality

requirements, but it will take longer to

produce it."

This way of thinking states that you can't achieve all three simultaneously. However, the Japanese automaker, Toyota, has shown that they can meet all three. Toyota is now able to produce a car from customer order date to delivery faster than any other auto manufacturer. Toyota is also able to maintain the lowest defect rate as measured in parts per million. They are cost competitive in any world market and can often command a premium price for their cars because of their speed and quality.

Remember, speed, cost and quality can be achieved together. If your team is able to make it happen, you will be well on your way to achieving a competitive advantage.

Inverting the Organizational Pyramid

Where do teams fit in today's organizational culture? Many companies are inverting the traditional pyramid, placing teams close to the customer and at the top of the pyramid. The types of teams discussed earlier will become the link to the customer. The new groups of teams being formed combine a company's employees with customers, end-users and suppliers. These teams are providing insights and specific suggestions for improving the quality of products and services delivered to the customer. Some examples of these teams are:

- Customer satisfaction teams

- Supplier quality-assessment teams

- Customer focus groups

- Partnerships or joint-venture teams

At the bottom of new organizations are the management teams. Two levels, the senior team and operational/functional heads, are responsible for strategy development and allocation of human and financial resources. In the past, senior managers were unable to make timely decisions because they were not linked closely enough to the needs of the customers.

Today, the teams closest to the customer are able to pass information directly to the management teams, quite often enabling immediate decisions. As a result, quality and speed increase, and customer satisfaction is enhanced. Teams are able to directly convert customer expectations into measurable objectives, which helps to manage the overall results of the organization.

INVERTING THE ORGANIZATIONAL PYRAMID

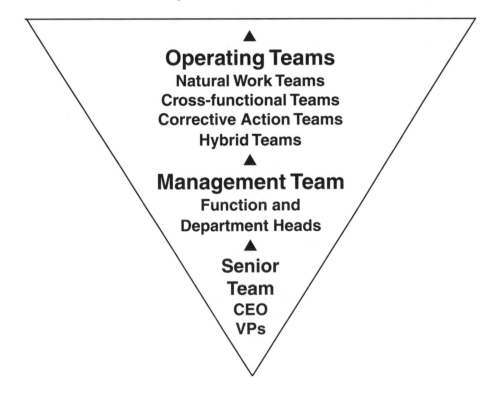

CUSTOMERS
▼
Customer Satisfaction Teams
Vendor Relationship Teams
Partnerships & Joint-Venture Teams

▲
Operating Teams
Natural Work Teams
Cross-functional Teams
Corrective Action Teams
Hybrid Teams
▲
Management Team
Function and
Department Heads
▲
Senior
Team
CEO
VPs

Getting Close to the Customer

It is essential that team members see their work through the eyes of their customers and know how customers actually use the products and feel about the services provided for them. Teams then gain greater appreciation of the customers' needs and new insights into how best to respond to them. The inverted pyramid represents an opportunity to increase your performance by receiving feedback directly from customers. Here's how some companies are inverting the pyramid.

1. Create visits to your customers and allow your employees to see customers actually using their products.

2. Videotape customers using your products and receiving your services. Then replay them during a team meeting.

3. Open communications; invite customers to team meetings. Listen for individuals' actual experiences in the customer-user chain.

4. Provide employees with access to company merchandise so they can experience the products firsthand. This could include company discount purchase plans.

5. Establish ongoing customer interfaces from concept and design through delivery. Surveys, rating sheets and phone interviews can be used most efficiently.

6. Create users' conferences, where your company sponsors meetings and invites users of its products and services. This is a great opportunity for team members to get feedback, as well as present additional information to users.

What Makes a Winning Team?

There are two main factors that will determine a team's effectiveness. The first is the task factor — the ability of the team to accomplish what it has committed to do through mutual goals. This is how the team's performance is measured. Teams invariably begin to tackle their task work immediately and often overlook the opportunity to create positive team dynamics, which support their performance.

The second factor in team effectiveness is relationships — where the team focuses on the one-to-one and intergroup dynamics that can help productivity by building collaboration.

As a team identifies what it needs to succeed, the team leader and members must take responsibility for developing a climate of trust. Even a simple exercise of getting to know each other's backgrounds and experiences can later help teams to delegate responsibilities to the right members. It is important to balance the task and relationship factors because this combination contributes to achieving speed, cost and quality improvements.

Keep in mind that a team with good relationships that does not perform is not considered successful. Likewise, teams that meet their goals but do not have positive relationships will not last over a long period of time. Team members do not have to "like" each other to get things done effectively. However, without a climate of mutual respect and support, teams have little hope of gaining a competitive advantage.

Think about these two factors as a process, with optimal results as the output.

Team Process

Task	+	Relationships	=	Optimal Results
(Performance)		(Interpersonal Dynamics)		

Learning to Mix Task and Relationship Behaviors

As just described, a balance of task and relationships will help a team optimize its results. Below are examples of specific behaviors relating to both tasks and relationships to help you understand what you can do for each.

Tasks: Actions done to accomplish goals

- Assigning work

- Presenting information

- Reviewing accomplishments

- Asserting one's view

- Decision-making

Relationships: Actions done to build interpersonal dynamics

- Clarifying work assignments

- Actively listening

- Recognizing effort

- Facilitating participation

- Reflecting on other values

- Collaborating

Identifying Your Task/Relationship Quotient

Think about participation of your current team or past teams. What behaviors do you exhibit most? Do you practice a balance of task and relationship behaviors in your current team?

To better identify your emphasis on task vs. relationship behaviors, rate yourself on the following actions.

Behavior	**Rating**
	(Seldom [1] - Always [5])
1. Motivating others to work on team goals	_____
2. Helping others to participate in team meetings	_____
3. Establishing good team relationships	_____
4. Focusing on deadlines	_____
5. Making sure people are heard	_____
6. Generating solutions and alternatives	_____
7. Managing and resolving conflicts	_____
8. Encouraging others to perform	_____
9. Managing time effectively	_____
10. Reinforcing good ideas	_____

Rating

Task Emphasis (add scores from 1, 4, 6, 8, 9) _____

Relationship Emphasis (add scores from 2, 3, 5, 7, 10) _____

You should strive to achieve balanced scores. If you find a large difference between your task and relationship functions, review the techniques in this handbook to help develop new behaviors. Then you must practice these new behaviors during your team meetings.

Benefits of Teams

Many of the companies that downsized their workforces over the past five years are still struggling to achieve the productivity advantages they hoped to realize. This is due, in part, to the fact that they have not found effective ways to maintain or boost productivity with fewer people. One of the potential benefits of teams is their ability to redistribute workloads, combine jobs and improve the workflow to get more accomplished with fewer resources.

There are benefits for you and others if you use effective teams. Consider the following benefits:

- You will be able to accomplish more by depending on the team to balance the workload during times of peak demand. Team members can be cross-trained to assume other jobs when needed.

- The opportunities for increases in job scope and responsibility will be numerous. You will be able to learn and perform new job duties and acquire the skills to excel. This will create growth and advancement opportunities.

- Teams will break down departmental barriers that have existed for many years. Not only will this make your work life easier, but it will make you more effective in meeting your goals.

- Rewards and recognition will vary from team to team. However, the value of team members will be recognized by customers and senior management. In certain situations, monetary rewards will be provided when a team has exceeded its goals.

- If teams can fill the gap left by downsizing, the most important benefit may be job security gained through customer satisfaction and loyalty.

Summary

Whether you are a team leader or team member, you have responsibility for contributing to the success of your team. By mastering the techniques of teamwork and achieving your team goals, you will be well on your way to creating a winning team. This success will "rub off" on other teams around you that are also struggling to find a winning formula.

2 CREATING POSITIVE TEAM DYNAMICS

Do the people at work frustrate you repeatedly? Do they disappoint you by not following through on commitments or upset you with insensitive comments? If so, you're not alone. Creating positive team dynamics with diverse people poses a significant challenge in today's workplace.

Individuals consider different values to be important. Some people believe "honesty is the best policy," while others might enjoy "playing company politics." Maybe you believe that information is power, something to be shared only with people who need to know. On the other hand, you might believe in being open with your co-workers, sharing your concerns and wanting to discuss them. Each of these is an example of a personal value, something that an individual considers to be important.

Team norms help team members know what is expected of them and how they can best work together. Team norms establish an acceptable "code of conduct," the way team members prefer to work together. When individual values match team norms, productivity and performance almost always increase!

As you are required to work on teams more frequently, you'll have opportunities to work more closely with more people than ever before. As a result, you'll frequently face the challenge of creating positive team dynamics. You'll be able to work better and more closely with your fellow team members if you identify common team values and norms.

Team Values

Team values are the beliefs that are important to all members. Values are rules that can dictate the behavior of individuals. A list of team members' values can be very long. However, a list of team values should be concise. The list is short because it is important that each member and the leader believe strongly in and are willing to live by the team values. The challenge for your team is to find the unique combination of values that the team supports but that also meet individual needs, so that each member follows them for the benefit of the entire team.

Identifying Team Values

To identify your team's values, start with the beliefs individuals say are important. Ask your teammates what is important to them; then write their responses on a piece of paper.

Examples of values

- Honesty — being truthful with others

- Quality — always striving to achieve the best results

- Friendliness with others — building positive relationships

- Thoroughness — completing whole jobs or projects

Once you have identified a list of what individuals say is important, have your team discuss it. Ask people if there are items listed that everyone believes are important. Create a list of your team's values by listing the items that everyone agrees are important. Once complete, look at the whole list of individuals' values again. Are there any values that your team should adopt even though each individual may not believe it is important at that moment? For example, some individuals may believe in the value "knowledge is power" and are thus unwilling to share information with others. Yet for the team to be successful, it may be necessary for everyone to communicate openly with each other. In this case, the team might adopt a value of open communication and encourage each member to share information with others.

Another consideration when identifying your team's values is what your company says is important. Many companies have created formal lists of values in recent years. Other companies have unwritten values, but an employee knows when she breaks them nonetheless. The employee might have the error pointed out or even be reprimanded for breaking a value.

What are your company's values? Are they formally written or simply "known" by everyone? You might find your company's values written in newsletters, on bulletin boards or on wall plaques. If you're unsure and can't find them, ask others what they believe your company's values are. Then make a list of your company's values.

When you have the list of company values, compare them to your team's values. Are there similarities? Significant differences? You may want to engage your team in a discussion about the comparison of team and company values. To be successful, your team's values have to support what the company believes is important. Establishing team values consistent with those of your company is important, but the true challenge is to get consistency across individual, team and company values!

One approach to getting consistency is to create a relatively small list of "core" values. Identifying core values is an attempt to enable each individual to accept and embrace the stated values of the team and company. The list of core values communicates what is fundamentally important to the company, to the team and to individuals. They help define acceptable behaviors for teams. Winning teams establish an effective balance between what individuals consider to be important and what is vital to everyone. The key to your team's success is to be tolerant of individual differences, yet consistent as a whole. For example, a team may believe strongly in meeting deadlines but may tolerate individual preferences for exactly when the work is done.

An example of a company making an effort to identify acceptable corporate, team and individual values is the Mexico facility of the Black & Decker Company, the worldwide manufacturer of power tools. They have identified four core values they use as a central focus for bringing together and directing the work of all employees.

All employees and teams within the facility are expected to adopt these values as their own. Everyone is expected to act in ways consistent with them. Having these core values helps ensure people are working together for their common benefit.

The four core values of the Black & Decker Company are:

1. **Integrity**

   - Treating customers, suppliers and employees with honesty, justice and a sense of doing what is right

   - Sharing respect with others

   - Making actions correspond with words

2. **Innovation**

   - Making an effort to improve products or service

   - Finding creative solutions and taking preventive measures

   - Searching for constant change and improvement

   - Avoiding repetition of errors

3. **Excellence**

   - Developing a sense of pride for a job well done

   - Supplying quality products and services on time

   - Comparing always with the best

   - Keeping promises

   - Maintaining high standards of professionalism

4. **Teamwork**

   - Listening carefully to others and showing a sincere intention

   - Sharing ideas in an open and honest manner

   - Guiding actions to reach team objectives

(Black & Decker Mexico, 1990)

Team Norms

Whether you know it or not, your team already has some norms. *Webster's Dictionary* defines norms as "principles of right action, binding upon the members of a group and serving to guide, control or regulate proper and acceptable behavior." Another way of saying the same thing is that norms provide guidelines for how people treat each other.

Some of your team's norms might be formal and planned, such as meeting every Tuesday or beginning every meeting on time. But think of how many norms have cropped up unofficially. To identify unofficial norms, consider:

- Who sits where in meetings?

- Who speaks first at meetings?

- Do some team members speak all of the time while others stay quiet?

- Do some members leave before meetings are over?

- Do people interrupt each other in meetings?

The answers to these questions indicate norms your team has adopted unofficially.

Norms are very powerful because they deal with the way people act. Without norms, everyone would probably act by their own guidelines without thinking about how their actions affect others. It would be hard for people to work together. Norms provide people with guidelines for choosing actions that are appropriate for different situations.

Since we spend most of our day with other people, we look to norms to guide us in our behavior. When you are at work you act by one set of norms, but when you are at a sports event you probably act by a different set. At a wedding you act differently than at a funeral. That's because there are different norms for different occasions and for different groups.

One problem with norms is that they are not always clear (Is it okay to speak now, or should I wait?). Another problem is that norms may be accidental or unplanned rather than planned. (Did anyone plan for people to cheer after our national anthem is played at a sports event?) For teams to work effectively, members must have norms that are clear and planned. Team success is too important to leave norms to chance.

Identifying Team Norms

Remember your team values? We said earlier that values are important because most of our actions, even if we don't know it, are dictated by our values. With your team values fresh in your mind, now focus your attention on developing a list of team norms. There should be a lot of discussion about team norms. Be sure everyone has the chance to add their ideas, suggestions and disagreements. The team should come to a consensus on the ways you will operate.

To identify norms for your team, do the following:

1. Have your team members brainstorm a list of team norms. At this point all ideas are welcome.

2. Thoroughly discuss each norm. Talk about the effects each will have on your team's work.

3. Mark any which everyone agrees will help the team and, therefore, should be kept.

4. Ask if there are any that were left out. Is there something about how you act during team meetings? Do you have norms about how you will make team decisions and deal with disagreements?

5. Add any norms that you agree are important to helping your team work together successfully.

Here are some examples of team norms:

- Starting and ending meetings on time

- No substitutions for members

- Rotating meeting leadership

- Maintaining confidentiality of what is shared or discussed

Discuss your team norms thoroughly, even if it takes a couple of meetings. Don't just speed through this discussion to get it done. When each team member feels that the list is well thought out and complete, go back and be sure each norm is clear. Does each one make sense? Will team members remember what each norm means? This is very important for the norms to be embraced and followed.

The length of the list is not important, only the content and what each norm means to your team. Some teams have norms that include seven to 10 items, while others have more than 30. Remember, the purpose of norms is to guide proper and acceptable behavior within your team. This is why having norms embraced by all team members is so important.

Gaining Commitment to Team Norms

When you have finished your list of team norms, it is important that you get an indication of the commitment for them within your team. If each team member won't follow the norms, they can't be of much use. Ideally each team member should be enthusiastic about following norms, believing they will help lead to success.

When you're finished identifying your norms, ask each team member the following question: *On a scale of 1 (low) to 10 (high), how committed are you personally to the team norms?*

It's important to ask each person separately because you want to hear from everyone. You want to have each person on the team publicly acknowledge buy-in and commitment to the team's norms. Beginning with this exercise, each person can be expected to live by the norms, and other team members can be expected to tell one team member when she isn't acting according to one of the norms.

If any team member indicates a commitment level of 8 or less, the team should talk about the response. Find out why the person has difficulty committing to the norms. Ask the person what is necessary to get total commitment, and then the team should "tweak" the norms as necessary. It is important here not to just outvote or overrule individuals. Winning teams have the buy-in and commitment of all members when it comes to their norms.

Self-Management

A beneficial outcome of having team norms is that they can become a tool for self-management by team members. Team members know immediately when they are following norms and when they are not. Other team members will not only be allowed to tell people when they are not following the norms, but they will be expected to tell people.

When you complete a list of norms, discuss whether each of the following statements is true.

- Our team norms were decided by us and were not dictated to us by others.

- Accountability for following the norms is 100 percent within this team, and no one else will "police" us on following them.

- We give each other "mutual permission" to take the norms seriously, honor them and follow them consistently.

- We must take responsibility for telling members when they break norms, using a firm but constructive approach.

- Each of us must model the norms for others, and each of us must avoid saying, "I'll follow the norms only if everyone else does."

By discussing each of these statements, you can build a sense of self-management in each member of your team. You will lay an important foundation for resolving conflict and building trust.

Team norms are only as good as each member of your team makes them. Here's how to get your team to follow them.

1. Copy your norms or have them printed.

2. Have each member sign around the border of the copy as an indication of commitment to following the norms and seeing that others on the team follow them too.

3. Post them in your team meeting area.

4. Occasionally have your team discuss the norms and whether people are following them. Make any necessary changes to the norms.

5. All team meetings should be evaluated, and one question that should be asked is whether team norms are effective.

6. Team norms should not be cast in concrete but should be seen as evolutionary. They are effective until we substitute a new one, and the team should always be looking for new or better norms. It's much easier to criticize and develop norms than it is to criticize team meetings and members!

Summary

Team values and norms provide a stable foundation for building positive relationships on teams. Values define what is important to you and what rules you expect team members to follow at work. Norms go one step further, describing specific guidelines each person is expected to follow when working with other team members. Winning teams identify and embrace values and norms that recognize individual preferences but define how the team needs to work together to be successful.

3 TEAM LIFE CYCLE

Once your team members have identified values and norms, how do you get them working together? You've probably seen at least one team whose members argue with each other constantly. Maybe you know of a team whose members won't even talk to each other. These are examples of teams stuck in chaos, conflict and turmoil, never reaching peak performance. If your team is suffering from these problems, or if you're working well but not at peak performance, this chapter will give you strategies to help your team reach peak performance.

So what will help your team reach peak performance? How long will it take for your team to reach its best performance level? What can you do to help facilitate becoming an effective team or speed the process? The answers lie in what your team does each time you meet, especially the first time. Just as a first impression between two people makes a lasting impact, so does the first impression members have of a team. Getting off to a successful first step will set an important precedent for your team throughout its existence. From the first meeting, your team's success is an evolutionary process.

From the first meeting, your team must use the proper mix of task and relationship behaviors to reach peak performance.

Task behaviors help a team accomplish its objectives or achieve desired goals. They help a team focus on getting results in an effective and efficient way. Examples are:

- Setting specific goals

- Determining a course of action, including deadlines and timelines

- Solving problems quickly

- Determining customer expectations

- Establishing quality standards

Relationship behaviors help a team build positive relationships through an effective and efficient climate — an environment where people can feel motivated, valued, appreciated and respected. Examples include:

- Learning the skills and abilities of other teammates

- Discussing how well the team is working together

- Providing feedback and coaching

- Resolving conflicts and encouraging collaboration

By using the correct mix of task and relationship behaviors at the appropriate times, your team can progress to its peak level of performance more quickly and with less difficulty. However, using the behaviors incorrectly will keep your team locked in chaos and stifle progress.

When task and relationship behaviors are used correctly, your team's evolution to peak performance can be tracked in four stages or a Team Life Cycle: Infant, Adolescent, Young Adult and Established Performer. These stages are analogous to human development. The issues and concerns people face in growing from children to adults are the same issues and concerns your team faces in its evolution.

Stages of a Team Life Cycle

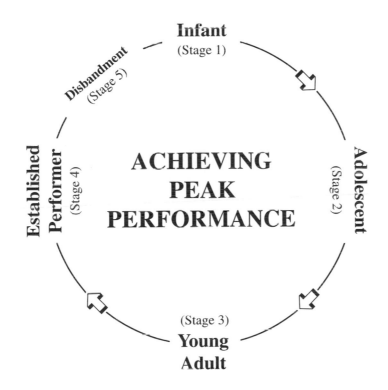

Stages of a Team Life Cycle Survey

Before we explore each stage of the team life cycle in more detail, complete the following survey. Your results will help pinpoint which stage your team is in. Then as you read this chapter, you can identify ways to help your team mature until you reach peak performance.

Instructions: Write the letters that correspond to how strongly you agree or disagree with each statement below. For instance, the first statement, if you strongly agree, write SA in the blank that follows the statement. If you slightly agree with the statement, write A, and so on.

Response Key:

SD = Strongly Disagree   A = Agree
D = Disagree   SA = Strongly Agree
N = Neither Agree nor Disagree

1. I know the goals my team is responsible for achieving. _____

2. Relevant information is generally shared among team members. _____

3. We have good rapport among team members. _____

4. Conflicts and unconstructive team member behaviors are confronted and resolved. _____

5. I know what is expected of me. _____

6. Team members cooperate with each other to solve problems and carry out decisions. _____

7. Team members communicate their ideas openly to each other. _____

8. Team members continuously find ways to improve how we do our work. _____

9. There is commitment from all members to being a high-performance team. _____

10. Morale on my team is high. _____

11. Team members trust each other. _____

12. Team productivity is generally high. _____

Scoring Your Survey Results

The Stages of a Team Life Cycle Survey provides two types of data for analysis: quantitative and qualitative. For quantitative data, a team total and team average are calculated for each question, using the following key:

$$SD = 1, \ D = 2, \ N = 3, \ A = 4, \ SA = 5$$

Determine the average for all questions, and use the following scale to interpret the results.

If the average is:

> *between 4 and 5:* Your team is working well together. You might consider fine tuning, but significant change is probably not necessary.

> *between 3 and 4:* Your team is working reasonably well. In a meeting, discuss members' top priorities and concerns, and brainstorm ideas for how your team can improve. Develop an action plan for improvement.

> *below 3:* Your team is not working well. In a meeting, have members choose their top two or three concerns, and brainstorm ideas for how your team can improve. Develop an action plan for each improvement area.

Qualitative data, such as comments, can be summarized and analyzed for each question as well. While no "magic formula" exists for this analysis, look for frequency and consistency among comments. Those comments mentioned most often or in several similar ways indicate a topic that should be discussed by your team.

In addition to providing both quantitative and qualitative data, the survey provides specific Stages of a Team Life Cycle results as well. Here are some specifics:

- *Questions 1 through 8* directly address concerns associated with the four Stages of a Team Life Cycle. Questions 1 and 5 address Infant concerns; 2 and 6 address Adolescent concerns; 3 and 7 address Young Adult concerns; and 4 and 8 address Established Performer concerns.

- *Questions 9 through 12* address your team climate. Morale can be measured over time. As your team progresses through the stages, results for these four categories should increase. Similarly, associated comments should also become increasingly positive.

When you have completed the analysis, use this agenda to discuss the results with your team.

1. Present the objectives and ground rules for the meeting.

2. Review Stages of a Team Life Cycle and information from this chapter.

3. Share survey data and answer questions.

4. Discuss and interpret results with your team.

5. Brainstorm team strengths and areas for improvement and prioritize them. (Subgroups may be formed to work independently.)

6. Solve problems within the top-priority area.

7. Identify and agree on action steps to improve the top-priority area.

8. Discuss next steps and set follow-up dates.

Stage One: Infant

How do you feel when you join a new team or take on a new or challenging project? Do you feel excited, enthusiastic, challenged or appreciative of the opportunity? Do you have a strong desire to do the job well? Maybe you're wondering who you'll be working with or exactly what you'll be doing. Whenever you join a new team or take on a new challenge, your team starts in stage one of its life cycle, the Infant.

The Infant stage is characterized by team members getting to know each other, learning the goals of the team and beginning to define their personal identities within the team. Members quickly set personal goals, determine what they want to get out of the experience and are polite in dealing with others. The team is completely dependent on authority for direction and support in this stage, just as an infant is dependent on its parents.

Infants epitomize dependence on others. Infants rely on others for feeding, care and love. Without this support, infants have little hope for continued growth and development. In return, infants offer enthusiasm, excitement and unconditional affection. They are eager to be cared for by others and willing to accept direction. Likewise, members of a team in the Infant stage are eager for direction and are initially willing to accept it without question.

In the Infant stage, team members demonstrate an enthusiasm and level of motivation higher than at any other time. This enthusiasm remains until the team moves to stage two. The transition between stages takes a short time (five to ten percent of the life of the team) if the team tasks are simple or a long time (as much as 60 percent of the life of the team) if the team tasks are complex. In stage one team members are willing to play and joke. However, in formal meetings they are stiff and tight-lipped, searching for acceptable team behavior.

Answer these questions to determine if your team is in the Infant stage.

- Are team members dependent on others for direction? (yes or no) What makes you think so?

- Are team members unfamiliar with others on your team? (yes or no) Have all members met each other?

- Do team members know their roles on the team? (yes or no) How clear are they?

- Are members inexperienced and unproductive? Do they need to learn how to improve their work? (yes or no) What evidence is there?

If you answered yes to these questions, your team could be in the Infant stage. Here are some strategies to help your team mature to stage two, the Adolescent stage.

- Request direction or clarity from senior management.

- Develop a team mission or set goals.

- Discuss team roles and responsibilities of individuals.

- Recognize enthusiasm and encourage members to keep it up.

During the Infant stage, it is imperative that your team focuses on both task and relationship behaviors, but emphasize task behaviors. Relationship issues exist; however, clarifying your team goals and plans take priority. Focusing on task behaviors helps you become productive more quickly, thus demonstrating success. Recognizing this productivity and success leads your team to the Adolescent stage.

Stage Two: Adolescent

Have you ever noticed people who purposefully avoid or ignore each other? Ever notice people who ignore conflict or try to cover up when team members are not getting along? Have you or your team members lost their enthusiasm for work? If so, you've seen or experienced people in the Adolescent stage of the team life cycle. This stage can be painful, one you want to progress through as quickly as possible, but usually cannot. The awkward aspects of personality and relationship development of teenagers in real life also plague work teams!

The Adolescent stage is characterized by conflict, confusion and lower team morale. The enthusiasm shown in the Infant stage disappears as members realize the difficulty of the team goals. This dip in morale results from the discrepancy between team member expectations and reality. Inexperience and lack of confidence seen in stage two behavior contribute to your team's inability to resolve conflict successfully.

Here are some examples of conflicts that arise in the Adolescent stage.

- Competing priorities

- Team members taking action without telling others

- Members not following team values or norms

- Members not meeting team standards for work completed

- Style or preference differences in how to complete certain tasks

- Unresolved tension and strained emotions

- Inadequate awareness of other team members' needs

- The formation of cliques and "special" friends

Adolescents or teenagers tend to resist authority, exercise their independence and learn through trial and error. They seem to thrive on chaos and conflict and seem willing to disagree just to spite others. Parents and outside observers usually find adolescents unpleasant, and they may even avoid them. However, a person cannot go directly from being an infant to an adult, no matter how much others may want them to avoid adolescence. The trials and tribulations of adolescence help individuals develop and mature, preparing them for adulthood.

In teams, the Adolescent stage is when members can learn from their mistakes, help resolve conflicts and begin to drive fear out of the team identity. Confidence and self-image form during stage two. A team must experience the Adolescent stage on its way to peak performance. However, the length of time a team stays in this stage varies widely and, for the most part, can be controlled. Keeping the team focused, planning for early and frequent successes and finding ways to discuss and resolve individual differences are ways members can help the team move through stage two more quickly.

Ask yourself these questions to determine if your team is in the Adolescent stage.

- Are members unhappy with their dependence on others? (yes or no) How do you know?

- Do they feel overwhelmed by the scope and difficulty of the team's task? (yes or no) Why?

- Do they openly display anger, conflict and dissension? (yes or no)

- Do individuals compete for status with other members? (yes or no) How?

- Do members openly challenge the team leader in meetings or in front of others? (yes or no)

41

If you answered yes to these questions, your team could be in the Adolescent stage. Here are some strategies to help your team mature to the Young Adult stage.

- Compare team goals and individual expectations; discuss differences openly.

- Plan for and then recognize team success early and often.

- Encourage people to take calculated risks and act without always asking for permission first.

- Identify conflicts among team members and address them.

- Recognize when mistakes are made; then treat them as opportunities to solve problems, discuss them and learn from the experience.

In the Adolescent stage you need to equally emphasize both task and relationship behaviors. Focusing on goals and making decisions helps the team continue to increase the level of productivity. Additionally, you must discuss and resolve conflicts, give feedback to each other, learn from mistakes and work to drive fear out of the team. Stage two is potentially the most painful for a team and subsequently requires the most effort. Once team members begin to address conflict effectively, they are ready to move to the Young Adult stage.

Stage Three: Young Adult

Have you ever been part of a team in which people trust each other, work hard and like being part of the effort? Perhaps your team is like this now. Are people asking for cross-training or requesting opportunities to take on new challenges? Occasionally, people may get upset with each other or feel they can't resolve problems with particular individuals. If your team is doing well, but you know you can get even better, your team is probably in stage three, Young Adult.

As a Young Adult team, the problems of conflict and confusion in the Adolescent stage have been overcome. Team members work together to complete the tasks at hand. Like the previous stages, the Young Adult stage can be quite short, even nonexistent, or very long in duration. Most teams get to this stage but then never move on to become Established Performers. In this stage, members should continue task behaviors, but now emphasize relationship behaviors — supporting each other, providing feedback and discussing conflicts that block them from becoming Established Performers. By now people have learned how to do the job required, but the team needs to emphasize positive relationships to be most successful.

Young adults tend to be self-confident and have a know-it-all mentality. This confidence is helpful because young adults learn primarily through trial and error. Learning fuels confidence, and results in a productive cycle. Likewise, team members in the Young Adult stage have high self-confidence as a result of surviving the chaos and conflict of the Adolescent stage. In many cases, team members still face the majority of the task ahead of them, yet they now have experience together and will help each other. Many members preserve team harmony at all costs, resisting conflict for the good of the team. As members become more willing to challenge each other, they become even more effective at recognizing and appreciating differences, resolving conflicts and completing tasks.

The key to teams moving through stage three to reach peak performance lies in the ability of members to develop norms and processes to work together and, at the same time, to value their individual differences. A paradox that occurs in stage three is that members may avoid conflict and hold back controversial ideas or avoid discussing differences for fear of losing team harmony, even though they have demonstrated an ability to resolve problems effectively.

Ask yourself these questions to determine if your team is in the Young Adult stage.

- Do team members have feelings of trust, harmony and respect for each other? (yes or no) How do they demonstrate their feelings?

- Do individuals demonstrate self-confidence in relating to others and in completing tasks? (yes or no) How?

- Has your team developed norms for working together and making decisions? (yes or no)

If you answered yes to these questions, your team could be in the Young Adult stage. Here are some strategies to help your team reach the next stage.

- Formalize team norms for making decisions, resolving conflicts, etc.

- Celebrate successes in task accomplishments and improved relationships.

- Recognize increases in levels of trust, confidence, etc.

- Begin cross-training of team members.

- Recognize the strengths of individuals on the team.

As your team members become more proficient and productive during the Young Adult stage, task focus becomes less important. Relationship behaviors become the priority. Members dedicate time and effort to providing feedback and encouragement, thus mending the relationships broken in the earlier stages. Members establish norms, enabling trust and respect to develop. As your team's harmony and cohesion increases, relationship behaviors reinforce open communication and trust among members. Your team is now ready to reach for peak performance, stage four.

Stage Four: Established Performer

Stage 4 is unlike any other stage. Members of teams that reach stage four demonstrate tremendous levels of productivity, autonomy, initiative and cohesion. An Established Performer team focuses primarily on getting work done. Having learned how to work together, overcome conflict and confusion and efficiently make decisions in earlier stages, team-member competence reaches its highest level.

Answer these questions to determine if your team is operating at peak performance.

- Are members working at their highest level of productivity? (yes or no) Why do you think so?

- Do members effectively acknowledge differences and resolve conflicts? (yes or no) How?

- Has your team experienced synergy, completing tasks more efficiently or effectively together than they could have as individuals? (yes or no) Provide examples.

If you answered yes to these questions, your team could be in the Established Performer stage. Here are some strategies to help your team remain at peak performance.

- Communicate openly and freely to all team members.

- Encourage autonomy and shared team leadership.

- Assign tasks to individuals and rotate responsibilities.

- Periodically review relationships and address issues as necessary.

Once your team reaches peak performance, emphasis on either task or relationship behaviors is not necessary unless problems arise. Members will tend to work autonomously for the benefit of the team, focusing on common goals while learning from each other. Team harmony and cohesion are strong. Teams can continue in this stage indefinitely without a lot of focused effort.

Stage Five: Disbandment

If your team has a specific, deliverable goal or a definite ending point, a fifth stage, Disbandment, exists. This is regardless of whether your team ever experienced being an Established Performer. When forming a team, it may be easier to get commitment from people if a specific ending date is known in advance. However, as the end date nears, team work is characterized by members being concerned by their inevitable termination. Members sometimes deny their feelings or try to hide them by joking or avoiding others on the team. In this stage you must acknowledge others' feelings, concerns and behaviors. By consciously raising people's feelings and dealing with them, you can help members leave the team believing it was a positive experience.

Teams can be looked at as living organisms, like people, that go through multiple stages of maturity. Teams that achieve peak performance are successful because of hard work and focus, not good fortune. The team life cycle provides a helpful framework to understand the phases a team must go through to reach peak performance.

The following graphic depicts the effects of the life cycle on a team's productivity and morale.

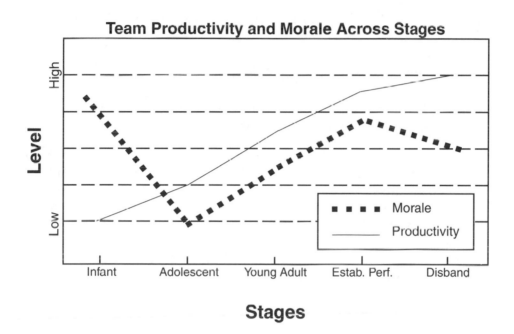

In stage one, the Infant, team-member morale starts very high and productivity is very low. The team struggles to define its identity, establish a mission, set clear goals and accomplish tasks. Nonetheless, members are enthusiastic and optimistic about the opportunity to be a part of the team.

In the Adolescent stage, team-member morale drops. The extent of the drop in morale can be very significant, depending on how effectively people react and whether members set and achieve milestones. As members learn more about the team goals and their individual responsibilities, productivity increases. Teams tend to experience conflict, grief and chaos during the Adolescent stage.

47

As a team reaches the Young Adult stage, members begin to work together and resolve conflicts effectively. Their productivity level continues to increase through this stage. Morale reverses its trend and begins to increase as well. Members establish norms for working together and begin to experience the benefits of synergy during the Young Adult stage.

As an Established Performer, a team reaches its highest level of productivity. Morale also reaches a higher level but may not reach the same level of enthusiasm as in the Infant stage. Members feel they are valuable to the team and contribute accordingly. They also act independently and take initiative freely, knowing that their fellow members are supportive.

For teams that experience the Disbandment stage, both productivity and morale can either increase or decrease. This depends on how individuals react to the team's inevitable end. In some cases, a lot of work remains, and individuals work harder to meet a deadline. In other cases, the team finishes early and does not work as hard as they near a deadline. If the experience has been positive, team members may be upbeat about their success, thereby projecting a positive morale. If the experience was not satisfactory, or if members are not looking forward to the end of the team, their morale may suffer.

Usually when teams experience special challenges or problems, they regress to earlier stages. For example, if a team in either the Young Adult or Established Performer stage replaces one or more members, it may revert to the Adolescent stage. Members will not know or feel comfortable with the new person(s). Conflict and problems could result. Teams that regress need to emphasize relationship behaviors. They need to help the new member(s) become a part of the team. Once done, the whole team will quickly progress to its previous stage.

Summary

Reaching the Established Performer stage is not automatic. The journey can be long and difficult, and some teams never make it. There are four stages along the way, with a fifth stage if the team has a definite ending date. Teams mature from Infants to Adolescents to Young Adults before becoming Established Performers. The fifth stage is Disbandment, when team members know their end is drawing near. Using the right combination of task and relationship behaviors at appropriate times is the key to becoming an Established Performer.

By understanding these behaviors and using them, you can help your team reach peak performance! You now have a variety of tools and strategies to address almost any situation you encounter on your team. Overcoming problems of conflict and chaos are difficult, yet necessary, if your team is to reach peak performance. With your courage and insight, you can use these strategies to help your team achieve success.

4 A SYSTEMATIC VIEW OF TEAMS

As teams become more predominant in the workplace, expectations of what teams can achieve grow. But there is a dilemma for many teams. They are failing to achieve their expected results. Often breakdowns in communication create frustration and loss of productivity. In fact, poorly organized teams are actually slowing down progress — the exact opposite of the desired outcome of quicker, better quality and lower-cost expectations!

Teams frequently begin in a frenetic and sometimes chaotic fashion. Members are quickly thrown together and assigned a task. Teams that get off to a disjointed start have the odds stacked against them for achieving successful results.

You can contribute to the success of your team whether you're a team leader or a team member. You can help guide your team to a more systematic view of your team's start-up and development. This will help your team avoid some of the stumbling blocks that historically have paralyzed teams. Think of the components of team development as building blocks to your future success. Use the components to guide your team through the maze of potential problems during your team's start-up and throughout your existence.

Teams may never become systematic. We may never be able to plan every detail to guarantee a team's success. However, by viewing teams systematically, you can use these guidelines to help your team be most productive.

Flow Chart

SYSTEMATIC VIEW OF TEAM DEVELOPMENT

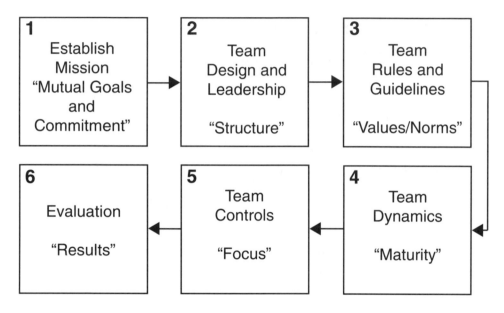

1
Establish
Mission
"Mutual Goals
and
Commitment"

2
Team
Design and
Leadership

"Structure"

3
Team
Rules and
Guidelines

"Values/Norms"

6
Evaluation

"Results"

5
Team
Controls

"Focus"

4
Team
Dynamics

"Maturity"

Key Components and Descriptions

1. Establish Mission … "Mutual Goals and Commitment" Having a common team mission and purpose is a key to achieving successful results. The mission must be established early in the formation of the team and then translated into achievable goals that all team members can clearly understand. The goals will help clarify the specific tasks for which the team will be responsible. The next step is identifying to whom the team is accountable in reporting its results. The team must then next commit to action by putting dates, times and personal responsibilities to the goals. This will provide accountability for the team's performance.

Here are some important questions to consider:

- Is your team clear about why you exist?

- Has a mission or purpose statement been prepared?

- Have your customers and suppliers been identified?

- Is there a reporting line for your team?

- Do individuals have a basis for developing their goals and role descriptions?

- Does your team know its boundaries in terms of decisions it can make?

Your team should discuss its mission. All team members must be clear about why the team exists to ensure commitment. Your team must also clarify who its customers and suppliers are and plan regular communications with them. It is never too late to begin this critical step. As a team member, you can help by encouraging your team to clarify its mission and to build strong links to your customers and suppliers.

2. Team Design and Leadership ... "Structure" The second component of the team system is to design the structure of the team. The structure should be based on team type. For example, in a natural work team, the work unit supervisor or manager would be the team leader, and everyone else would be members. In a cross-functional team, the leader might be someone representing the function that would benefit from the team's work, and members would represent all functions involved. In a corrective-action team, the team leader might be someone with the most knowledge of the problem to be solved, and members might be others who are interested in participating. Ad-hoc team members may be selected randomly from volunteers, and an individual may accept team leadership as a developmental opportunity. In each case, the team leader and team members were specifically chosen and assigned their roles. Effective teams are not simply groups of individuals thrown together. Rather, they are individuals who each play a critical role in the team's success.

Here are some important questions to consider:

- Is your team clear on where it "fits" in your organization?

- Has your team contacted customers and suppliers for input on your mission or project?

- Have team member selection criteria been identified?

- Is the role of team leader clearly known by your team?

- Is there a progress assessment available to help identify improvement areas?

As a team leader or member, you can help your team to clarify the structure. Identify the team leader, and list the responsibilities of that person. Consider your membership — do you have the appropriate people on your team? Helping the team understand its overall role in the organization will help gain commitment from members and from the beneficiaries of your team's efforts.

3. Team Rules and Guidelines … "Values/Norms" One of the most important teambuilding blocks is to immediately establish the rules and guidelines that will guide behavior and interpersonal dynamics. By focusing on team values and norms, you set the standards for the life of the team. It is critical that team members participate in the establishment of the values and norms, because they become committed to them. The values and norms should be consistent with those of the company.

Here are some important questions to consider:

- Does your company have stated values?

- Are these values understood and accepted by your team?

- Do team members know each other, including backgrounds?

- Have norms or guidelines been established for your team?

- Do team members agree to abide by these norms?

- Are your team members' roles clear?

- Does your team have a commitment to self-management?

If your team has not established its values or norms, you may want to bring in an experienced facilitator to help you through this critical process. Facilitators can be anyone outside of your team who can remain neutral. By keeping the discussion focused, this resource person can help guide your team through establishing its values and norms.

If members seem unsure, discussions regarding role clarification (who will do what?), team membership (are the right people on the team?) and team leadership (who is the leader?) will prove beneficial. By setting values and norms and discussing team membership and leadership, your team will be on its way to peak performance.

4. Team Dynamics ... "Maturity" In this component, the team life cycle or stages of maturity are identified by the team. The ideal situation occurs when the team is able to move from its Infant Stage to one of Established Performer. These techniques will help the team mature more quickly and gain commitments to team guidelines, rules and goals. It will also help to overcome inevitable conflicts and chaos as the team moves toward peak performance.

Here are some important questions to consider:

- Do team members understand the team life cycle?

- Has your team identified its current stage of maturity?

- Has your team discussed any techniques to increase its movement toward being an Established Performer?

- Does your team periodically review and monitor its values and norms?

- How does your team deal with lack of adherence to values and norms?

Simply by knowing where your team is in its life cycle, you can anticipate and minimize potential problems. You can recommend preventive or corrective actions to avoid or overcome the problems. Your role can be very critical in helping your team mature into an Established Performer.

5. Team Controls … "Focus" The next component requires the team to establish methods of assessing performance, using agreed upon measurements. This component requires a clear understanding of the team goals and of the potential reward and recognition opportunities. Much of the success of the team will depend on how much responsibility can be delegated to team members. If members are clear about their roles and how they contribute to the overall success of the team, an empowering climate will be created. Individuals will begin to take initiative to solve problems and complete tasks without being asked. The focus of team control can then shift from the leader to the individual members. By taking initiative and measuring results, team members will begin to recognize achievements and increase their motivation and performance to even higher levels.

Here are some important questions to consider:

- Have team performance measurements been established?

- How will your team know if it has been successful?

- What types of rewards and recognition will be provided for your team?

- How does your team measure progress and communicate the results?

- Are team members empowered to take immediate action?

- How will your team build on its effectiveness and teamwork?

Everyone on the team should take responsibility for its performance. You can conduct ongoing assessments of how you are progressing toward your goals. You can encourage others to do the same. If you are a team member, ask your team leader to help. Together, the two of you can initiate periodic team progress reviews. This will help create a sense of team ownership.

6. Evaluation ... "Results" The measure of success depends on whether the team achieves desired results. An evaluation of the team's output is conducted by an assessment of both its customers and management sponsors. The team itself conducts a final evaluation and determines "lessons learned" as part of its disbandment. This applies most often to corrective-action and hybrid teams. Team members can then pass these lessons on to other existing teams or ones that are just starting up in the organization.

Here are some important questions to be considered:

- What tools will be used to assess team performance?

- Will both team and individual results be rewarded?

- What frequency of evaluation will apply?

- Who will conduct the evaluations?

- How will these evaluations be utilized by similar teams to increase their productivity?

- What must change to support the systematic team view?

By encouraging frequent evaluations of performance, you can help your team achieve its desired results. One process you might suggest is the peer review. In this process, team members are encouraged to give feedback to others on how well they see each individual performing. This can be done in a face-to-face team meeting, or you can use questionnaires that team members complete about each other. The questionnaires are then summarized and the results distributed to individuals. You can also begin to collect feedback from your customers. Again, this can be done face-to-face or through a written mechanism. Many teams use a return post card. The card is sent to customers, and, when completed, it is returned to the team.

Regardless of how you collect performance information, this is one of the most important steps you can take to help your team be successful. By knowing what others think of your work and how well you're meeting goals, you can recognize deficiencies and begin to correct them. In this way, feedback provides positive, helpful information. It is information you will want to collect and consider.

Paving the Way for the Team System

No matter how well your team is organized, three important characteristics must be present to pave the way for your team's success.

- **External Relations**: the interactions with other individuals or groups

- **Work Systems**: flexible job responsibilities that support cross-training

- **Policies and Procedures**: guidelines that determine recognition, rewards and work schedules

How a team can improve its external relations

No matter how a team has established its team rules, mission and responsibilities, its success will be limited if it lacks relationships outside of team membership. Relationships with other teams, individuals and departments are critical to accomplishing a team's mission.

A good team will constantly communicate with its customers and suppliers to ensure that the team mission is accepted. Your suppliers need to know what is expected. The more clearly their roles are identified, the more likely vendors will act and be responsible for your desired outcomes. Every team member must take responsibility to ensure that external relationships are managed effectively.

Team actions to ensure positive external relations

- Make sure that all decisions and actions of the team are communicated and understood by everyone affected by your team's output.

- Continually seek out ways of working effectively with other teams and departments. Remain cooperative.

- Use outside speakers and contacts as a source of ideas and comparisons.

- Set up joint meetings in which issues can be aired.

- Set up joint training sessions with other departments. Mixing the visions and strategies of work groups stimulates action.

How a team can improve its work systems

For team members to work effectively, individuals should review their job descriptions and make sure that they are completely accurate and up-to-date. Team members must share their job descriptions with each other and cross-train wherever possible.

Team members must be able to redesign their work processes to improve productivity. Redesign and reengineering occurs naturally when team members share responsibilities and commit to meeting each others' goals. Opportunities abound for increased efficiency and improved effectiveness from this shared perception. These opportunities may be based on customer requirements and should be immediately discussed with the team leader to gain support for implementation. Here are some actions team members can take to improve work systems.

- Constantly seek opportunities to decrease cycle times for the tasks for which you are responsible.

- Seek opportunities to cross-train with your team members and be a resource for them.

- Seek training opportunities, including both in-house and outside seminars, to improve problem-solving skills.

How a team can improve policies and procedures

Team members can impact and improve only policies and procedures that are within their control. To help reshape traditional policies and procedures, the team must identify how it wants to be recognized, especially in nonmonetary ways.

The team can also help modify the appraisal process by encouraging peer reviews to help determine performance ratings.

In fact, one of the best strategies for building team productivity and increasing performance is to evaluate everything. For example, consider customer ratings of jobs that are completed. The team can also request flexible work schedules to make better use of resources and to meet individual needs. But don't just adjust work schedules; look for opportunities to maximize your time and create new opportunities to see your team from new perspectives.

Actions to improve policies and procedures

- Request a feasibility review of job sharing, flex-time, profit-sharing and team incentives by your human resources department.

- Suggest how the team will be recognized if it exceeds its goals.

- Make suggestions for improving work rules, e.g., overtime, distribution of workload and delegation of responsibilities.

Summary

Winning teams are developed with a systematic approach to their formation and ongoing development. Each component is a building block toward the overall success of the team.

Outside forces are also important to the support and success of a team. Ongoing communications with other teams, customers and suppliers will ensure that your team is proceeding in the right direction and on the way toward achieving its desired results.

5 VALUING INDIVIDUAL DIFFERENCES

People are different. This is a simple statement, rarely questioned and generally taken as a given in today's work environment. Yet identifying and, perhaps more importantly, valuing individual differences has only recently become relevant.

Some differences among people are obvious from the first time you meet them. Others are discovered only after you've known one another for some time. There's nothing that will heighten personality differences and behavior quirks faster than working together on a team. There are numerous individual differences you'll encounter on teams. However, if you want to build positive relationships, there are four types of differences to consider:

- Interpersonal styles

- Personal work styles

- Experience and background

- Communication styles

Interpersonal Styles

Whether a person talks fast, uses hand gestures or withdraws quietly — these are examples of interpersonal style differences. Other examples include if a person asks you about your family or personal life or if another person doesn't even say hello in the morning. The way we see a person interacting with others helps us identify the individual's interpersonal style.

Interpersonal styles can reflect individual personalities too. You probably know at least a couple of people who don't get along because their personalities clash. Our personalities play a big part in determining team effectiveness. How a person approaches someone else and whether that person is friendly or not have a big impact on how effectively you will work together.

One key to building strong relationships on your team is to make sure members get to know and feel comfortable working with each other. This goes beyond members simply telling each other their names and a little bit about themselves. To move toward peak performance, members need to build trust and confidence in each other, or they'll never take calculated risks. Opening up, sharing information and insights and constructively challenging others' opinions are difficult for teams if individuals don't feel comfortable with each other.

One way to get everyone started on working together is to identify skills, abilities, past successes and individual accomplishments. Build a team brag file and don't be afraid to use it!

Personal Work Styles

Some people like to plan their work, creating checklists to ensure everything gets done. Others appear less organized, working without an obvious plan. Some people wait until the last moment; others get work done well in advance of deadlines. You may know someone who arrives to work very early or stays very late. All of these are examples of how individuals approach work differently. These differences can be particularly troublesome for teams, especially when people have to work closely. Sustaining individuality in a team setting can be very trying.

Another difference in people's personal work styles is how they set priorities. We all like to do certain tasks and don't like others, and we may not appreciate how our actions affect others around us. As a result, we may set priorities for ourselves that are not consistent with others' needs. These individual preferences and conflicting priorities — our personal workstyles — make it difficult to work well with some people.

Experience and Background

Have you ever worked with a 20-year veteran and a new recruit? If so, you've probably witnessed the kinds of differences attributed to experience. Veterans may be locked into certain ways of completing tasks, unwilling to consider new ideas. New recruits may want to change everything, not taking into consideration the wisdom of the past or the effect on others around them. Some people have college degrees; others learned skills on-the-job. Our individual experiences and backgrounds are almost always different from others at work. As a result, we approach work differently and question the methods of others around us. One essential ingredient for team effectiveness is being able to blend past successes with strong, new perspectives.

Communication

Another particularly troublesome difference you may have identified on your team is communication styles — how people get information to others. Communication styles vary with each individual. Here are some examples:

- *Silence* — Not everyone feels a need to talk. For many people, to pause or be silent indicates thinking and consideration.

- *Non-verbal communication* — Most easily misinterpreted, this type of communication is most effective when individuals are familiar with each other. If misinterpreted, your gestures will not enhance clarity.

- *Pointing out problems and resolving conflicts* — Some people will confront others directly and constructively. However, others may simply agree to avoid confrontation and reduce conflict.

- *Identifying hot buttons* — We all have particular topics we prefer not to discuss. If mentioned, we may get upset or even angry. To communicate effectively, you must identify the hot buttons of others and then find ways to avoid them or gently treat them in team discussions.

So what's the significance of these differences? As you are asked to participate more frequently on teams, your success will be increasingly dependent on your ability to work well with people who are different than you. Working effectively with people who are different will be essential! However, the differences mentioned here only scratch the surface of what you'll encounter on teams. What other types of differences can you think of among members of your team?

Recognizing Differences on Your Team

An important part of building strong relationships on your team is effectively resolving problems with others. The first step is to recognize the various differences that exist on your team. At your next team meeting, use the differences mentioned previously. See how many styles you can find among your teammates. Then consider these questions:

- Did you recognize differences in each of the types mentioned? Can you accommodate for personality differences?

- What communications differences did you see? Are there ways you can anticipate problems before "crunch time" hits your project?

- What differences do you personally bring to your team? Are there obvious strengths or glaring holes that can be patched?

- Do the differences you've identified help or hinder your team?

- How can these differences be used to strengthen your team?

Once you've identified differences, engage your team in a discussion about them. Solicit examples of how differences have helped or hindered this team or others in the past. Brainstorm ideas about how the team can benefit by building on individual differences, and identify ways you can implement any ideas the whole team believes will be beneficial.

Identifying differences among your team members is only part of the challenge. Building on those differences to create a winning team spirit is important. Successful teams get results because of the people, not in spite of them. Successful teams, plain and simple, have positive relationships. The quality of the relationships gives teams a sense of cohesion, a key ingredient to achieving synergy.

Team cohesion

Enhancing the sense of cohesion is essential. Every productive team member has a sense of connectedness and identity. Knowing you are included in the team gives you a sense of belonging and confidence so you can make a meaningful contribution. On the other hand, feeling different and having that difference reinforced by subtle exclusion lead to a decrease in your participation and productivity.

Here are five suggestions to improve the cohesion of your team.

1. When your team first forms, be certain to state that everyone present is an integral part of your success and that everyone is to be included in all discussions and activities.

2. Try to notice one team member who seems to be on the fringes of a conversation, and pull that person in by asking him to comment on the discussion.

3. After a meeting, approach a person who seems to be a bit removed from your team and speak to that individual in a friendly and personal way. Then comment on how much of a contribution he makes. Every team member should know, recognize and affirm other team members' competency. But sometimes that happens only when it's deliberately planned.

4. Find an opportunity to have lunch or coffee with people who appear to need reinforcement. Let them know they are valued members of the team.

5. If members of the team informally plan to meet for a social gathering after work, be certain everyone is invited.

* NOTE: Each of these suggestions was once the responsibility of managers, supervisors, bosses or team leaders. But not anymore! Every team member must share in the responsibility for establishing and maintaining team cohesion.

Worst-case scenario: if you're the only one taking the responsibility for team cohesion, you'll build an identity for yourself, and other team members will feel better. Best-case scenario: others will join in, and that's when high-performance teams really work.

It takes an effort to make everyone on a team feel a sense of cohesion. With work teams today, it is easy for individual differences to lead to barriers and unintentional conflict. Feeling comfortable with only those who are most like yourself is a reflection of old habits that need to be changed. Sit and talk with those who are different and include them in discussions to build a sense of total team perspective. Team cohesion directly leads to strong relationships, which ultimately points to success!

Personal commitment

Even if people feel comfortable working with each other, a sense of team cohesion and positive relationships takes effort. Positive relationships need nurturing and care. As the reader of this book, you're in a very favorable position to help your team become more successful. To gain momentum, you must start with yourself.

Do you feel comfortable working with others on your team? How good are the relationships you have with other team members? Are there a lot of differences among your team or specifically between you and others? What have you done to improve relationships on your team? We've given you ideas and techniques to help build positive relationships, but you must have the personal commitment to succeed.

Personal commitment is not situational. If you want positive relationships, you must work toward them, regardless of whether others are helping. Use the techniques we've provided. Keep a positive attitude. Recognize every success, and your efforts will be rewarded. You'll be a big part of building a winning team.

Summary

Individual differences on teams are inevitable. Identifying differences, discussing them and getting to know others will help your team build a sense of cohesion. The final ingredient needed is personal commitment, your relentless pursuit of success. Remember, winning teams not only accomplish their desired tasks, they build positive relationships too.

6 AVOIDING TEAM FAILURE

Given all the information provided thus far, there is still a chance your team could fail in its efforts. In the "real world," teams do not always have the opportunity to do all the right things that will guide them to success.

Often teams are put together without considering what will determine their success. In cases like this, there are common pitfalls that teams experience:

- A lack of principles for effective teamwork

- Having ineffective meetings

- An inability to give effective feedback

- Not having a climate for mutual respect

If you find yourself in this type of situation, the ideas in this chapter will prove useful to you and your team.

Case Study

It is your first team meeting. You received a memo last week from a department director that asked for your participation on a problem-solving team. There wasn't much detail about what you were expected to do, nor was an agenda included.

As the other team members arrived, you recognized only a few of the participants. Your team leader, Jerry, started the meeting quickly. He did most of the talking, skipping introductions because he assumed most participants knew each other. Jerry didn't really think that was important because he viewed his job as "getting on with the work." He discussed the overall project but seemed confused about what the team's responsibility was. Many questions went unanswered. The basic premise — that everyone was there for the same reason — was lost in Jerry's emphasis on finishing the meeting before the one-hour time allotment expired.

Most of the participants left the meeting frustrated. You are concerned about the future of this project and the level of success that can really be achieved. Given the pitfalls previously mentioned, consider the following questions:

- As a conscientious team member, what might you suggest to Jerry to help him build a more solid foundation for this new team?

- What would you do during the next meeting to encourage more team interaction?

In this example, Jerry has fallen into several of the pitfalls that lead to team failure. We'll look at each pitfall in more detail and identify ways to avoid each.

Avoiding Pitfall #1: Establish Principles of Teamwork

Teamwork and team synergy are achieved when the output of the team is greater than the actions of the individual team members. The formula of 2+2=5 applies to a team that has developed superior teamwork.

One of the tools used by effective teams is developing a set of principles that help create a positive environment during team meetings. If you are a team leader, you will want to model these principles each time you meet with team members individually or in a group situation. If you are a team member, you will want to try these tactics during team meetings. This is an excellent opportunity to begin creating a climate of openness and trust. The following principles will facilitate effective teamwork.

Focus on the behavior, not the person

A natural tendency when teams are in conflict is for members to focus their criticism on an individual and not the issue or behavior at hand. Consider these tips to have a more positive impact.

- It is important that you assess the specific behavior and not the person in general. Separate the person from the problem and always solve the problem first! Generally, the people issues will work themselves out if you fix the right problem. If not, you know the next action is a personnel issue.

- Avoid using all-encompassing phrases like "you never ..." or "you always ..." These phrases are not behavior-specific and often put people on the defensive. If you cannot describe the problem in 11 words or less, you're not ready to discuss the solution. The discussion should focus on solving the problem — not "airing" all the faults.

Stress the positive

A natural tendency is to focus on what went wrong. Although this input is critical for continuous improvement, try to balance your comments.

- Make it your practice to provide positive comments along with suggestions for improvement. Think about leading with the positive and then covering critical points.

- It is far more important for team members to move from problems to solutions than to blame and justify each event. Three simple questions can help you grow in spite of problems.

  1. What did we learn?

  2. What opportunities exist now?

  3. Who will be responsible for getting us back on track?

Be specific and sincere

The only way feedback can be effective is if your comments are specific and to the point. Your team members will know if you are sincere. Be sure to use clear examples to illustrate what you're concerned about, and have a definite idea of what you think must be done to correct the problem. Do not expect other team members to have hundreds of ideas to contribute — you've thought about it, they haven't.

Once you have laid out a path for corrective action, step aside and let the team modify it. Try not to focus on the "right" things to do; stay focused on your desired outcome.

Express confidence

Be sure to let the team know that you are confident in its ability to produce results. Let members know that you support the team decision-making process and consensus building. Consider using sentences that begin with "I feel" or "I think." This technique will encourage other team members to respond in the same way and will help to foster honest and open communication.

Avoiding Pitfall #2: Conduct Effective Meetings

All teams need to communicate through meetings. Whether they are one-on-one encounters, a small group of three or four members or a whole team gathering together at one time, meetings are the lifeblood for effective teams. Information must flow from the leader to the members, from members to other members and into and out of the team. That transfer of information happens in meetings.

So if meetings are so important, and we go to so many of them, why are the ones we have so poor? Frankly, most people don't consider the importance or benefits that can be gained by having effective meetings. Furthermore, most people don't plan and prepare for their meetings, and too few understand the characteristics of an effective meeting. Simply put, people believe meetings are a nuisance either to be avoided or kept to a minimum at all costs.

The reality is, however, meetings may be the most important ingredient to team success. We've already discussed the value of having mutual goals and commitment, of effectively resolving conflicts and of getting everyone involved in problem-solving. With teams, these actions happen primarily in meetings.

Review the Case Study at the beginning of this chapter. One reason people may be leaving the meeting frustrated or confused is because of the poor quality of the meeting. With a few changes, Jerry's meeting could be much more effective and have more positive outcomes. So what are the characteristics of effective meetings? There are four:

1. ***Be prepared.*** Meetings can be a waste of time if everyone is there, but everyone is not ready. Whatever the topic of the meeting, be sure that everyone is prepared. If information is to be shared, have it there in advance. If a problem is being analyzed, have all the necessary documentation available to help the team. There is no substitute for being prepared! Don't just show up — show up ready to make a contribution.

2. ***Have the right people in the meeting.*** Part of being prepared is also having the right people in the meeting. If you've ever been to a meeting where a critical person was missing, chances are you know the frustration that results. If you need a person to help make a decision, provide information or present a different point of view, be sure that individual attends the meeting. Otherwise, the meeting can be a waste of time. One practice worth considering is to cover all meetings with another person who represents your interests. And, the representative has total authority to say yes or no in your absence.

3. ***Have an agenda.*** Tell everyone the purpose of the meeting. Furthermore, tell everyone what will happen in the meeting. If the purpose of the meeting is to make a decision, let everyone know immediately what that decision is. Similarly, if the purpose is to communicate information, let people know that as well. By having an agenda and communicating it to participants up front, people have a better chance to come prepared. The meeting will flow more evenly and efficiently. It works best to circulate the agenda beforehand, but, at a minimum, circulate and announce the agenda as soon as the meeting begins.

4. *Have individuals take responsibility.* At the end of the meeting, have individuals take responsibility for action steps. In every case, meetings should result in decisions and actions that need to be implemented. If there is not a next step involved, you should probably not have held a meeting. By having individuals take responsibility, team members will know who is accountable for what and when action should be taken. Include in this part who will take responsibility for organizing the next meeting. This way, the team can rotate or share meeting leadership responsibilities and ensure that the next meeting will go well.

One thing people need to see modeled is volunteering for action. Take every opportunity to build a "can-do" and "I will do" tone, and others will follow.

Using these four principles of effective meetings is not difficult, but the benefits will be significant. You'll recognize changes almost immediately. By being prepared, having an agenda and having the right participants in the meeting, your team can communicate effectively and gain the commitment it will need to be successful.

Avoiding Pitfall #3: Giving and Getting Effective Feedback

No one likes hearing that their performance is less than adequate or not what was expected. Accordingly, there is nothing more difficult than having to tell people that their work or behavior is unacceptable. Yet the ability to give feedback effectively is one of the most important team skills for members to possess.

Feedback can be either positive or constructive. The purpose of positive feedback is to recognize behavior and encourage it to happen again. Constructive feedback helps people understand the negative effects of their behavior and what could be done differently. When someone helps you solve a complex problem, the feedback you offer shows your appreciation and encourages the other person to help you again the next time you need it. On the other hand, when someone does something that upsets or frustrates you, telling that person can be the best way to make sure it doesn't happen again.

Consider the Case Study at the beginning of this chapter. How would you tell Jerry your feelings about the meeting? How can you make suggestions to Jerry without upsetting him, or worse, having him retaliate in some way? There are five things to keep in mind when you have to give constructive feedback.

1. ***Be specific.*** Feedback is helpful only when the other person knows exactly what she did. If feedback is too general, the receiver may misinterpret the message or not understand. As a result, the message may be ignored, and nothing will change.

2. ***Speak for yourself.*** You must offer feedback from your experience. It's not uncommon for team members to tell you how another person has upset them. They may even ask you to talk to the other person for them. However, feedback is most effective when it is given directly to the person involved. Offer feedback when you need to, and encourage other team members to do the same. Make every attempt to stifle speaking for others.

3. ***Share your feelings.*** Telling another person how specific actions make you feel can be a powerful message. Sometimes people simply don't know the impact of their actions. Sharing your feelings may encourage other people to change their behavior.

4. ***Emphasize the effects on you.*** As with feelings, sometimes people don't understand how their behavior affects others. When someone's behavior causes you problems, tell that person. More times than not, she will appreciate the message and change the behavior as a result. Most people don't know your priorities. Since only you truly know your projects, the best way to reduce stress and

the negative impact of others is to let them know the consequences of their behavior.

5. *Use the "I" technique.* The "I" technique is a straightforward approach to giving effective feedback. The format of an I message is:

I feel ... (your feelings) when you ... (specific actions) because ... (effects)

Start the feedback message with your feelings. If you're frustrated, angry or anxious, tell the other person right at the beginning. Follow your feelings with a specific description of the other person's behavior. Keep this brief; emphasize only one or two behaviors. Otherwise, your message could be perceived as a lecture. Finish the message by describing the effects of the behavior on you. Here are two examples:

I feel strongly that our effectiveness is reduced when you are not at team meetings, because we lose the benefit of your insight and experience.

I get worried when you don't keep me informed about what is happening in your area, and I start imagining problems you may be having.

Giving feedback, especially constructive feedback, can be very difficult. However, the "I" technique can help make giving feedback much easier. Practice giving feedback with your team members. As with any skill, practice will help you give more effective feedback.

Avoiding Pitfall #4: Developing a Climate of Mutual Respect

Not all members of teams become the "best of friends," nor should they. The goal of a team is productivity, not friendship! However, if a climate of trust and mutual respect is not established, the ability of the team to interact honestly and openly will be impeded. The lack of mutual respect will ultimately affect how quickly the team can resolve problems through sharing of information.

One easily learned technique for gaining the mutual respect of your team members is to engage in active listening. This technique will help you do two things:

- Understand the other person's point of view

- Have a genuine interest and empathy for the other person

What is active listening?

Active listening is the ability to hear a message clearly, using your eyes and ears, with complete concentration. Consider these techniques:

- Prepare to listen by sending listening signals.

    Welcoming signals show that you want to talk to the person.

    Attention signals — both vocal and nonverbal — show that you are listening ("hmm," nod your head, etc.).

- Control distractions, which are barriers to listening.

    Examples include looking away, shifting objects, yawning, sitting at a distance, answering the phone, tapping a pencil, etc.

- Listen to the entire message, and take time to listen and probe for information. Try these:

    "Tell me more."

    "What else should I know?"

    "What makes this so important?"

    "How did this situation come about?"

    "For example?"

- Reinforce the communication by sending verbal and nonverbal cues that you are listening. Some of these are:

    Nodding your head

    Using hand gestures

    Maintaining eye contact

    Saying "uh-huh"

- Confirm the message by playing it back. Use phrases like these:

    "If I understand you correctly ..."

    "I hear you saying that ..."

    "So, what happened is ..."

    "The situation, then, is ..."

- Here's an easy-to-follow active listening script:

Step 1 — Make direct eye contact, take a deep breath and say, "I want to hear everything you have to say, so please take your time."

Step 2 — At some point, the other person will stop and assess your level of interest. At that point, make direct eye contact and say, "Is that all? Is there anything else you want me to hear?"

Step 3 — Wait quietly.

Summary

The stage is set for teams to fill the gap left by change, including re-structuring and downsizing. Teams have more responsibility than ever before to contribute to the success of the organization. Much of this responsibility will fall on the shoulders of the individual team members who must work together.

As a team member, you will be responsible for ensuring that you clearly understand the goals of the team, as well as your individual role and performance plan. You must also make an effort to build relationships that support positive team dynamics.

Use the tools available to you to help meet both the task and relation-ship building factors that contribute to building winning teams. Your goal will be to help your team perform the tasks required, relying on a climate of mutual respect and the ability to value individual contributions.

In the organizations of the future, there will be less bureaucracy and less dependence on higher-level managers. Consider yourself one of the critical success factors in building winning teams in this new environment.

Reading List

Anderson, Karen. *To Meet or Not to Meet.* Overland Park, KS: National Press Publications, 1992.

Belasco, James A. *Teaching the Elephant to Dance.* New York: Penguin Group, 1991.

Blanchard, Kenneth, and Spencer Johnson. *The One-Minute Manager Builds High-Performing Teams.* New York: Morrow, 1991.

Buchholz, Steve and Thomas Roth. *Creating the High Performance Team.* New York: John Wiley and Sons, 1987.

Cairo, Jim. *The Power of Effective Listening* (four-cassette album). Overland Park, KS: National Press Publications, 1989.

Dubrin, Andrew J. *Stand Out.* Englewood Cliffs, NJ: Prentice-Hall, 1993.

Dugger, Jim. *Listen Up: Hear What's Really Being Said.* Overland Park, KS: National Press Publications, 1991.

Goldratt, Eliyahu and Jeff Cox. *The Goal — A Process of Ongoing Improvement.* New York: North River Press, 1986.

Hackman, J. Richard, ed. *Groups That Work (and Those That Don't): Creating Conditions for Better Teamwork.* San Francisco: Jossey-Bass, 1990.

Hendricks, Bill. *Project Management* (audiocassette album). Overland Park, KS: National Press Publications, 1991.

Isgar, Thomas. *The Ten-Minute Team: How Team Leaders Can Build High Performing Teams.* Boulder, CO: Seluera Project, 1989.

Ketchum, Lyman, and Eric Trist. *All Teams Are Not Created Equal: How Employee Empowerment Really Works*. New York: Sage Publications, 1992.

Lahey, Richard. *Teamwork Counts*. Buffalo, NY: Dok Publications, 1991.

Larson, Carl E., and Frank M.J. Lafasto. *Teamwork: What Must Go Right, What Can Go Wrong*. New York: Sage Publications, 1989.

Mallory, Charles. *Team-Building*. Overland Park, KS: National Press Publications, 1989.

Meyer, Chris. E.. *Fast Cycle Times*. New York: The Free Press, 1993.

Nora, John J., C. Raymond Rogers, and Robert J. Stramy. *Transforming the Workplace*. Princeton, NJ: Princeton Research Press, 1986.

Shaw, M.E. *Group Dynamics: The Psychology of Small Group Behavior* (3rd ed). New York: McGraw-Hill, 1981.

Torres, Cresencio and Jerry Spiegel. *Self-Directed Work Teams, a Primer*. San Diego: Pfeiffer and Company, 1991.

Weisbord, Marvin R. *Productive Workplaces*. San Francisco: Jossey-Bass, Inc., 1987.

Wellins, R.S., W.C. Byham, and J.M. Wilson. *Empowered Teams*. San Francisco: Jossey-Bass, 1991.

Wilson, Patricia. *Empowering the Self-Directed Team*. Overland Park, KS: National Press Publications, 1993.

INDEX

H

Hot buttons, 66
Hybrid teams, 2, 12, 57

I

Individual differences, 63-70
        Communication styles, 63, 66
        Experience and background, 63, 65
        Interpersonal styles, 63, 64
        Personal work styles, 63, 65
Infant stage, 33, 38, 39, 47
Information, 5
Interpersonal dynamics, 14, 54
Interpersonal styles, 63, 64
Inverted pyramid, 11-13
"I" technique, 79

J

Job descriptions, 60
Joint-ventures, 11, 12

L

Layoffs, 1
Leadership, 55, 77
Levels of authority, 4

M

Management teams, 11, 12
Maturity, 52, 55
Mayo, Elton, 3
McGregor, Douglas, 3
Meeting agendas, 72, 76

Meetings, 58, 59, 71, 72, 75-77
Morale, 47
Mutual respect, 14, 71, 80

N

Natual work teams, 2, 12, 53
Nonverbal communication, 66
Norms, 24-29, 52, 54-56

O

Organizational culture, 11
Organizational pyramid, 11, 12

P

Partnerships, 11, 12
Peak performance, 31-34, 44, 46, 55, 64
Peer reviews, 58
Personal commitment, 69
Personal work styles, 63, 65
Pitfalls to avoiding team failure, 72, 82
    Number one: establish principles of teamwork, 73, 74
    Number two: conduct effective feedback, 75-77
    Number three: giving and getting effective feedback, 77-79
    Number four: developing a climate of mutual respect, 80-82
Policies and procedures, 58, 60, 61
Problem-solving, 5, 72
Productivity, 2, 5, 47, 80
Products, 11

Q

Qualitative data, 36, 37
Quality, 2, 9-11
Quantitative data, 36, 37

R

S

T

Buy any 3, get 1 FREE!

Get a 60-Minute Training Series™ Handbook FREE ($12.95 value) when you buy any three. See back of order form for full selection of titles.

These are helpful how-to books for you, your employees and co-workers. Add to your library. Use for new-employee training, brown-bag seminars, promotion gifts and more. Choose from many popular titles on a variety of lifestyle, communication, productivity and leadership topics. Exclusively from National Press Publications.

Buy more, save more!
BUY 3, GET 1 FREE!

DESKTOP HANDBOOK ORDER FORM

Ordering is easy:

1. Complete both sides of this Order Form, detach, and mail, fax or phone your order to:

   Mail: National Press Publications
   6901 W. 63rd St.
   P.O. Box 2949
   Shawnee Mission, KS 66201-1349

   Fax: 1-913-432-0824

   Phone: 1-800-258-7248 (in Canada 1-800-685-4142)

2. Please print:

Name _____ Position/Title _____

Company/Organization _____

Address _____ City _____

State/Province _____ ZIP/Postal Code _____

Telephone (___) _____ Fax (___) _____

3. Easy payment:

❏ Enclosed is my check or money order for $_____ (total from back).
Please make payable to National Press Publications.

Please charge to:
❏ MasterCard   ❏ VISA   ❏ American Express

Credit Card No. _____ Exp. Date _____

Signature X _____

• •

MORE WAYS TO SAVE:

SAVE 34%!!! BUY 20-50 COPIES of any title ... pay just $8.50 each ($10.95 Canadian).
SAVE 42%!!! BUY 51 COPIES OR MORE of any title ... pay just $7.50 each ($9.95 Canadian).

Buy 3 get 1 FREE!
60-MINUTE TRAINING SERIES™ HANDBOOKS

TITLE	RETAIL PRICE	YOUR PRICE	QTY.	TOTAL
8 Steps for Highly Effective Negotiations #424	$12.95	$9.95		
Assertiveness #442	$12.95	$9.95		
Balancing Career and Family #415	$12.95	$9.95		
Change: Coping with Tomorrow Today #421	$12.95	$9.95		
Customer Service: The Key ... Customers #488	$12.95	$9.95		
Dynamic Communication Skills for Women #413	$12.95	$9.95		
Empowering the Self-Directed Team #422	$12.95	$9.95		
Getting Things Done #411	$12.95	$9.95		
How to Conduct Win-Win Perf. Appraisals #423	$12.95	$9.95		
How to Manage Conflict #495	$12.95	$9.95		
How to Manage Your Boss #4982	$12.95	$9.95		
Listen Up: Hear What's Really Being Said #4172	$12.95	$9.95		
Managing Our Differences #412	$12.95	$9.95		
Master Microsoft® Word #406	$12.95	$9.95		
Motivation and Goal-Setting #4962	$12.95	$9.95		
A New Attitude #4432	$12.95	$9.95		
PC Survival Guide #407	$12.95	$9.95		
Parenting: Ward & June ... #486	$12.95	$9.95		
Peak Performance #469	$12.95	$9.95		
The Polished Professional #426	$12.95	$9.95		
Powerful Leadership Skills for Women #463	$12.95	$9.95		
Powerful Presentation Skills #461	$12.95	$9.95		
The Power of Innovative Thinking #428	$12.95	$9.95		
Real Men Don't Vacuum #416	$12.95	$9.95		
Self-Esteem: The Power to Be Your Best #4642	$12.95	$9.95		
SELF Profile #403	$12.95	$9.95		
The Stress Management Handbook #4842	$12.95	$9.95		
Supreme Teams: How to Make Teams Work #4303	$12.95	$9.95		
The Supervisor's Handbook #410	$12.95	$9.95		
Team-Building #494	$12.95	$9.95		
Techniques of Effective Telephone Comm. #429	$12.95	$9.95		
Techniques to Improve Your Writing Skills #460	$12.95	$9.95		
Total Quality Management #418	$12.95	$9.95		
The Write Stuff #414	$12.95	$9.95		

Sales Tax		
All purchases subject to state and local sales tax. Questions? Call **1-800-258-7248**	**Subtotal**	$
	Add 7% Sales Tax *(Or add appropriate state and local tax)*	$
	Shipping and Handling *($1 one item; 50¢ each additional item)*	$
	Total	$

VIP No. 705-008438-096

Buy any 3, get 1 FREE!

Get a 60-Minute Training Series™ Handbook FREE ($12.95 value) when you buy any three. See back of order form for full selection of titles.

These are helpful how-to books for you, your employees and co-workers. Add to your library. Use for new-employee training, brown-bag seminars, promotion gifts and more. Choose from many popular titles on a variety of lifestyle, communication, productivity and leadership topics. Exclusively from National Press Publications.

DESKTOP HANDBOOK ORDER FORM

Ordering is easy:

1. Complete both sides of this Order Form, detach, and mail, fax or phone your order to:

    Mail: National Press Publications
    6901 W. 63rd St.
    P.O. Box 2949
    Shawnee Mission, KS 66201-1349

    Fax: 1-913-432-0824

    Phone: 1-800-258-7248 (in Canada 1-800-685-4142)

2. Please print:

Name _____ Position/Title _____

Company/Organization _____

Address _____ City _____

State/Province _____ ZIP/Postal Code _____

Telephone (___) _____ Fax (___) _____

3. Easy payment:

❑ Enclosed is my check or money order for $_____ (total from back).
Please make payable to National Press Publications.

Please charge to:
❑ MasterCard   ❑ VISA   ❑ American Express

Credit Card No. _____ Exp. Date _____

Signature X _____

• •

MORE WAYS TO SAVE:

SAVE 34%!!! BUY 20-50 COPIES of any title ... pay just $8.50 each ($10.95 Canadian).
SAVE 42%!!! BUY 51 COPIES OR MORE of any title ... pay just $7.50 each ($9.95 Canadian).

Buy 3 get 1 FREE!
60-MINUTE TRAINING SERIES™ HANDBOOKS

TITLE	RETAIL PRICE	YOUR PRICE	QTY.	TOTAL
8 Steps for Highly Effective Negotiations #424	$12.95	$9.95		
Assertiveness #442	$12.95	$9.95		
Balancing Career and Family #415	$12.95	$9.95		
Change: Coping with Tomorrow Today #421	$12.95	$9.95		
Customer Service: The Key ... Customers #488	$12.95	$9.95		
Dynamic Communication Skills for Women #413	$12.95	$9.95		
Empowering the Self-Directed Team #422	$12.95	$9.95		
Getting Things Done #411	$12.95	$9.95		
How to Conduct Win-Win Perf. Appraisals #423	$12.95	$9.95		
How to Manage Conflict #495	$12.95	$9.95		
How to Manage Your Boss #4982	$12.95	$9.95		
Listen Up: Hear What's Really Being Said #4172	$12.95	$9.95		
Managing Our Differences #412	$12.95	$9.95		
Master Microsoft® Word #406	$12.95	$9.95		
Motivation and Goal-Setting #4962	$12.95	$9.95		
A New Attitude #4432	$12.95	$9.95		
PC Survival Guide #407	$12.95	$9.95		
Parenting: Ward & June ... #486	$12.95	$9.95		
Peak Performance #469	$12.95	$9.95		
The Polished Professional #426	$12.95	$9.95		
Powerful Leadership Skills for Women #463	$12.95	$9.95		
Powerful Presentation Skills #461	$12.95	$9.95		
The Power of Innovative Thinking #428	$12.95	$9.95		
Real Men Don't Vacuum #416	$12.95	$9.95		
Self-Esteem: The Power to Be Your Best #4642	$12.95	$9.95		
SELF Profile #403	$12.95	$9.95		
The Stress Management Handbook #4842	$12.95	$9.95		
Supreme Teams: How to Make Teams Work #4303	$12.95	$9.95		
The Supervisor's Handbook #410	$12.95	$9.95		
Team-Building #494	$12.95	$9.95		
Techniques of Effective Telephone Comm. #429	$12.95	$9.95		
Techniques to Improve Your Writing Skills #460	$12.95	$9.95		
Total Quality Management #418	$12.95	$9.95		
The Write Stuff #414	$12.95	$9.95		

Sales Tax
All purchases subject to
state and local sales tax.
Questions?
Call
1-800-258-7248

Subtotal	$
Add 7% Sales Tax *(Or add appropriate state and local tax)*	$
Shipping and Handling *($1 one item; 50¢ each additional item)*	$
Total	$

VIP No. 705-008438-096